# ELECTING LEADERS

## A CITIZEN'S GUIDE

Published in the United States of America by Cherry Lake Publishing
Ann Arbor, Michigan
www.cherrylakepublishing.com

Content Advisor: Austin McCoy, Doctoral Candidate in History at the University of Michigan
Reading Advisors: Marla Conn MS, Ed., Literacy specialist, Read-Ability, Inc.

Photo Credits: © Joseph Sohm/Shutterstock, cover, 1, 6, 9, 13, 27; © Lisa F. Young/Shutterstock, 5;
© Pressmaster/Shutterstock, 10; © DW labs Incorporated/Shutterstock, 14; © Africa Studio/Shutterstock, 19;
© Teresa Azevedo/Shutterstock, 20; © antb/Shutterstock, 22; © wavebreakmedia/Shutterstock, 24;
© BlueSkyImage/Shutterstock, 26; © Chris Parypa Photography/Shutterstock, 28

Library of Congress Cataloging-in-Publication Data
Names: Mara, Wil, author.
Title: Electing leaders / Wil Mara.
Description: Ann Arbor, Michigan : Cherry Lake Publishing, 2017. | Series: A citizen's guide |
    Audience: Grade 4-6. | Includes bibliographical references and index.
Identifiers: LCCN 2016001526| ISBN 9781634710664 (hardcover) | ISBN 9781634711654 (pdf) |
    ISBN 9781634712644 (pbk.) | ISBN 9781634713634 (ebook)
Subjects: LCSH: Elections—United States--Juvenile literature. | Political candidates—United States—Juvenile literature. |
Political campaigns—United States—Juvenile literature.
Classification: LCC JK1978 .M3638 2017 | DDC 324.70973—dc23
LC record available at http://lccn.loc.gov/2016001526

Cherry Lake Publishing would like to acknowledge the work of the Partnership for 21st Century Learning.
Please visit *www.p21.org* for more information.

Printed in the United States of America
Corporate Graphics

## ABOUT THE AUTHOR

Wil Mara is an award-winning and best-selling author of more than 150 books, many of which are educational titles for young readers. Further information about his work can be found at www.wilmara.com.

# TABLE OF CONTENTS

# Choosing Leaders

**O**ne of the most important days in America is known as **Election** Day. This day is truly a lasting statement of the power of **democracy**. Millions of people take part in the governing process through their right to choose their political leaders. They do this by voting. A vote is cast through a **ballot**, which is submitted at a location known as a **polling place**. For most people, the polling place will be reasonably close to their home.

Sometimes an election is held for a local political **office**. Examples of such an office include the positions of mayor, judge, city council member, or school board member in a specific town or city. There may even be a position open for the local dogcatcher!

People vote using ballots. Some places use paper slips, but most are counted electronically.

Barack Obama campaigns for the 2008 presidential election, which he eventually won.

Other elections are held at the state level. The most important and powerful position is the state's governor. There are other elected positions for each state, including senators, representatives, and judges.

Finally, there are national elections for positions in our federal government. The one you probably know best is for the office of President of the United States. Every four years—and always during a leap year—in November, an election is held for a new president. It can be a very exciting event. On those nights, the votes are counted on television as the whole nation watches. And while there is a kind of dramatic, almost theatrical, aspect to it, the fact is that it's the end result of a very long and complex process. Regardless of how important or powerful the position may be, electing a leader is a long, difficult process. It requires a group of dedicated and determined people, months and sometimes years of organizing and planning, and more hard work than you might imagine. It takes a great deal of teamwork from both volunteers and paid professionals to make a political **campaign** a success.

## Life and Career Skills

*To be a successful politician, even in local government, you need to spend time campaigning. This means connecting with the people who will be casting their votes—either for you or for the person running against you! You will need to convince the voters that you'll be able to help make their lives better. Successful politicians are charming, present themselves well, know how to give a strong speech, and take the time to listen to voters in order to learn their greatest concerns.*

# What Makes a Good Candidate?

**A**ll jobs require a certain set of skills, talents, and traits, both personal and professional. Think about it. Can a very shy person be successful in sales? Can someone who hates dealing with numbers have any hope of building a career as an accountant? The same principles apply to political **candidates**. If they don't have what it takes, they probably won't get very far. So, what qualities make a good candidate?

There are certain requirements a candidate must meet to run for office in the first place. These must-haves vary depending on the political office being sought. Most local governments require that a candidate be at least 18 years old. At the federal level, however, the requirements become quite a bit tougher.

The Republican candidates line up for a debate ahead of the 2016 presidential election.

In order to run for the U.S. House of Representatives, you must be:

- At least 25 years old

- A U.S. citizen for at least seven years

- A resident of the state in which you are hoping to be elected

To run for the U.S. Senate, you must be:

- At least 30 years old

- A citizen of the United States for at least nine years

- A resident of the state in which you are hoping to be elected

How a politician interacts with other people is key to his or her success.

To run for president, you must be:

- At least 35 years old
- A natural-born citizen of the United States
- A resident of the United States for at least 14 years

Aside from these requirements, there are critical personality traits that will make one person a better candidate than another. He or she should have a passion for helping others, because voters are counting on that person to improve their lives. Thus, the best candidates have a great deal of heart and commitment. Other traits include strong organizational skills, a willingness to work hard, tireless determination, and a positive attitude. This last one is much more important than you might think, because the candidate needs to stay upbeat when things go wrong. In the world of politics, they most definitely will!

## 21st Century Content

*New York Congressman Emanuel Celler served in the U.S. House of Representatives for half a century and faced just about every political challenge one can imagine. Summing up all the experiences of his profession, he once said, "One must have the friendliness of a child, the enthusiasm of a teenager, the assurance of a college boy, the curiosity of a cat, and the good humor of an idiot." That's quite a broad range of traits for one person to carry at all times. But it illustrates how pointless it is for someone too serious and uptight to have any hope of succeeding in public office.*

# The Importance of Teamwork

The work required to get elected into any political office is tremendous. Behind every campaign is a group of people who are just as dedicated as the candidate him- or herself, and each member of such a team has an important job. A campaign team can be just a few people, such as for a smaller local position. Or the team may include tens of thousands of people, which is typical if you're trying to help elect the next president of the United States!

The campaign manager oversees the entire campaign process. This person holds what may be the team's most essential and demanding position. He or she assigns responsibilities to the other campaign workers, determines the candidate's schedule,

People attend rallies to show their support for candidates.

Candidates use interviews to explain their ideas to the public.

and creates the overall campaign "vision." This includes the tactics the candidate will use to secure as many votes as possible. Decisions have to be made about what **issues** to emphasize, what groups of people to target, and which geographic areas to visit. The latter is particularly important because a candidate can't waste time visiting places where there is a very little chance of gaining votes.

A campaign manager usually has many helpers who are experts in different areas. They will have in-depth knowledge about specific issues that voters care about, such as immigration or health care. These **consultants** will help the candidate work out a policy on each issue so that the candidate can discuss it intelligently with the voters. A consultant may also have skills dealing with the **media**. This helps ensure that the candidate doesn't look like a fool in front of reporters for outlets such as television, radio, newspapers, and the Internet. A media consultant may also develop advertisements for these outlets, and that can be a tricky task in itself. A real pro in this area will know not only the right things to say in a political ad, but also how best

## 21st Century Content

Campaign finance laws were passed to prevent any person or group from "buying" a candidate by donating a lot of money to that person's campaign. This donation would assure that the person or group would receive some kind of favored treatment once the candidate was in office. Other campaign finance laws require detailed reports of how donations are spent. So the treasurer is accountable to not just the candidate but also the American taxpayer.

to say them, when to say them, and where each ad needs to run. Then there's the **pollster**—someone who knows how to run a survey in order to find out what's on the public's mind. The information a pollster brings to a campaign may affect everything from the creation of media ads to a candidate's position on key issues.

A treasurer deals with the campaign's **budget**. He or she has to be aware of every penny that comes in and goes out. But the job is not just about writing checks and accepting donations.

## Life and Career Skills

*Choosing to volunteer on a political campaign is a major commitment. The hours can be very long, the work can be demanding, and you may have to accept being one of the "unsung heroes" if your candidate wins the election. That means your name won't be singled out when the winner thanks his team. Also, never forget that being a volunteer means just that: you won't be getting paid for your efforts. With that in mind, what are some of the other reasons you might be willing to take on such a responsibility?*

There are strict laws about how much money can be donated to a campaign. The treasurer needs to know those laws inside and out and make sure the campaign doesn't break them.

Volunteers are among the most important people on a campaign team. They are the ones who willingly put in countless hours licking envelopes, answering phones, folding brochures, and doing other tedious but important tasks. They put up lawn signs, tie brochures to doorknobs, make coffee, and work at campaign events (sometimes in the evenings and on weekends). And they do all of this without pay because they believe the candidate will make their town, state, or country a better place. Volunteers are truly amazing people, and every candidate knows that without them, their campaign would go nowhere.

# On the Campaign Trail

**G**etting voters to know a candidate is a complex job. The purpose of a campaign is to introduce the candidate to the public in every way—his or her face, personality, background, credibility, policies, opinions, and so on. The campaign team has to figure out how to do this in a fairly short span of time and make the most of every opportunity. There are basically three ways that a campaign will present its candidate to the public. Let's take a look at each.

The first way to present the candidate is to focus on the candidate's political positions. What does he or she believe? Getting this information out there involves the candidate explaining his or her views on the issues that hold the highest

A candidate needs to have strong public speaking skills.

People sometimes show support for their favorite candidates by wearing campiagn buttons.

importance to the average voter. For example, the economy—matters relating to jobs and money—is always going to be a big one. The candidate will connect with the public through speaking appearances, press conferences, interviews, and so on. A candidate with good speaking skills, a solid sense of **diplomacy**, and a degree of personal **charisma** is better positioned to succeed in this effort.

The second way is to make the candidate's name visible in public places. The campaign team will give out freebies to basically everyone they can. These include shirts, buttons, hats, pens, magnets, yard signs, and bumper stickers with the candidate's name. Studies have shown that the more times people see a candidate's name, the more likely they are to vote for that person. The campaign team also aligns the candidate with special interest groups, raises money, and gets support or **endorsements** from important individuals and organizations.

Spreading the word about a candidate is most effective when done through the media. This involves getting either the

## 21st Century Content

*Never underestimate the importance of a candidate's visual appeal when it comes to an election. One of the most famous presidents in recent history, John F. Kennedy, was well known for his good looks. But he was actually trailing in the polls behind his opponent, Richard M. Nixon, for a long time. All that changed when he and Nixon faced each other on September 26, 1960, in the first candidates' debate ever shown on television. Kennedy was neatly combed and dressed, while Nixon looked haggard and tired. From that night on, Kennedy's poll numbers began to rise.*

Some candidates film campaign ads that run on television.

candidate or some other influential person on television, radio, or the Internet or in a newspaper or magazine. Advertisements are vital to any campaign. Some ads are sent directly through the mail to people's homes, while others are recorded messages sent by telephone. Campaigns may also make use of billboards on busy roads.

Campaign **slogans** are a fascinating part of political history. It's truly amazing what effect just a few carefully crafted words can have on the average voter. One of the most famous came from the campaign of Dwight D. Eisenhower. He was widely known by his nickname "Ike," and the slogan for his campaign became "I Like Ike." (It must have worked, because he won in a landslide!) Another slogan, from the campaign of Bill Clinton in 1992, was, "It's the economy, stupid!" This one worked because so many Americans were struggling to make enough money and Clinton's opponent, President George H. W. Bush, didn't seem to realize it. Clinton went on to win that election and then a second term in 1996.

During election season, candidates' teams make phone calls asking people to vote.

# Honoring the People Who Put You There

**P**resident Harry S. Truman once said the following about holding political office: "There is no life or occupation in which a man can find a greater opportunity to serve his community and his country." Most of the people who are elected to office today would agree. And it's important to remember that getting elected is just the starting point.

From the mayor of the tiniest town in America to the U.S. president, there are certain elements of the job that should always be honored. Anyone elected to office must be prepared to be part of a big team. A mayor must work closely with the chief of police, the fire commissioner, and the city council. The President of the United States must work alongside members of Congress, the

Politicians often have to make tough choices.

Politicians use the media to communicate with the people they represent.

Supreme Court, and his own cabinet in order to ensure that the nation's best interests are served. They all must spend the government's money, which they received from the taxpayers (such as your parents), wisely. They must address issues that weigh heavily on the voters' minds—everything from crime and unemployment to traffic congestion, foreign nations that don't like us, and a hundred other things.

Most importantly, an elected official must know how to lead. Crises come in a variety of shapes and sizes—economic downturns, international tensions, **infrastructure** breakdowns,

After Hurricane Sandy in 2012, many politicians visited the affected area to talk to residents.

hurricanes, droughts, terrorist attacks. The people elected to office are expected to not just face these challenges with us, but create the solutions to them.

This is why electing leaders is such a critical job. And that's where we, the voters, play our most important role.

## Life and Career Skills

*When we get involved with a political campaign, it's because our ultimate objective is to see our candidate win the election. But what about the things that can go wrong? For example, what if the media found out that your candidate cheated on his income taxes 10 years ago? Obviously voters wouldn't be too thrilled with the idea of voting for someone dishonest. How do you, as someone on the candidate's campaign team, think such a situation would be best handled? When the candidate turns to you for advice, what would you tell him or her?*

# Think About It

Imagine your candidate's campaign budget has enough money left for one more 30-second television commercial. The channels that would run it guarantee an audience of about 10 million voters. And let's also say that Election Day is coming up fast—maybe only a week away—and your candidate and his opponent are running neck and neck. What would you make that 30-second commercial about? Considering it could make or break the whole campaign, what message would you send to those voters?

Do you live in a "blue state" (Democrats) or "red state" (Republicans)? How did your state vote for president in the 2016 election? Did that party win or lose? Go online to find out about past election years. Does your state vote the same way every presidential election or has it changed over the years?

# For More Information

## BOOKS

Cunningham, Kevin. *How Political Campaigns and Elections Work*. Edina, MN: ABDO, 2015.

Goodman, Susan E., and Elwood Smith (illustrator). *See How They Run: Campaign Dreams, Election Schemes, and the Race to the White House*. New York: Bloomsbury, 2012.

Winter, Jonah, and Barry Blitt (illustrator). *The Founding Fathers! The Horse-Ridin', Fiddle-Playin', Book-Readin', Gun-Totin' Gentlemen Who Started America*. New York: Atheneum, 2015.

## ON THE WEB

**Congress for Kids—Elections: Political Parties**
www.congressforkids.net/Elections_politicalparties.htm

**Kids.gov—Government**
https://kids.usa.gov/government/index.shtml

**PBS Parents—Helping Kids Understand the Election**
http://www.pbs.org/parents/special/election/article-theraceison.html

# GLOSSARY

**ballot** (BAL-uht) a way of voting secretly, using a machine or slips of paper

**budget** (BUHJ-it) a plan for how much money you will earn and spend during a particular period of time

**campaign** (kam-PAYN) organized action in order to achieve a particular goal

**candidates** (KAN-di-dates) people who are running for office in an election

**charisma** (kuh-RIZ-muh) a powerful personal appeal that attracts a great number of people

**consultants** (kuhn-SUHL-tuhnts) experts in a particular field who are hired by others to give advice

**democracy** (dih-MAH-kruh-see) a form of government in which the people choose their leaders in elections

**diplomacy** (dip-LOH-muh-cee) being tactful and good at dealing with people

**election** (ih-LEK-shuhn) the act of choosing someone or deciding something by voting

**endorsements** (en-DORS-muhnts) support or approval of someone or something by other people or groups

**infrastructure** (IN-fruh-struk-shur) the basic things and systems that are needed for a place to function properly

**issues** (ISH-ooz) main topics for debates or decisions

**media** (MEE-dee-uh) ways of communicating information to large numbers of people

**office** (AW-fis) an important position of authority or power

**polling place** (POHL-ing plase) the place where votes are cast and recorded during an election

**pollster** (POHL-stur) someone who conducts a poll or compiles data obtained by a poll

**slogans** (SLOH-guhnz) phrases or mottos used by businesses, groups, or individuals to express a goal or belief

# INDEX